Between Rain, Wind, and Sun

Over the Edge with Oil Pastels

at the Ness of Brodgar

All within a sketchbook —Jeanne Bouza Rose

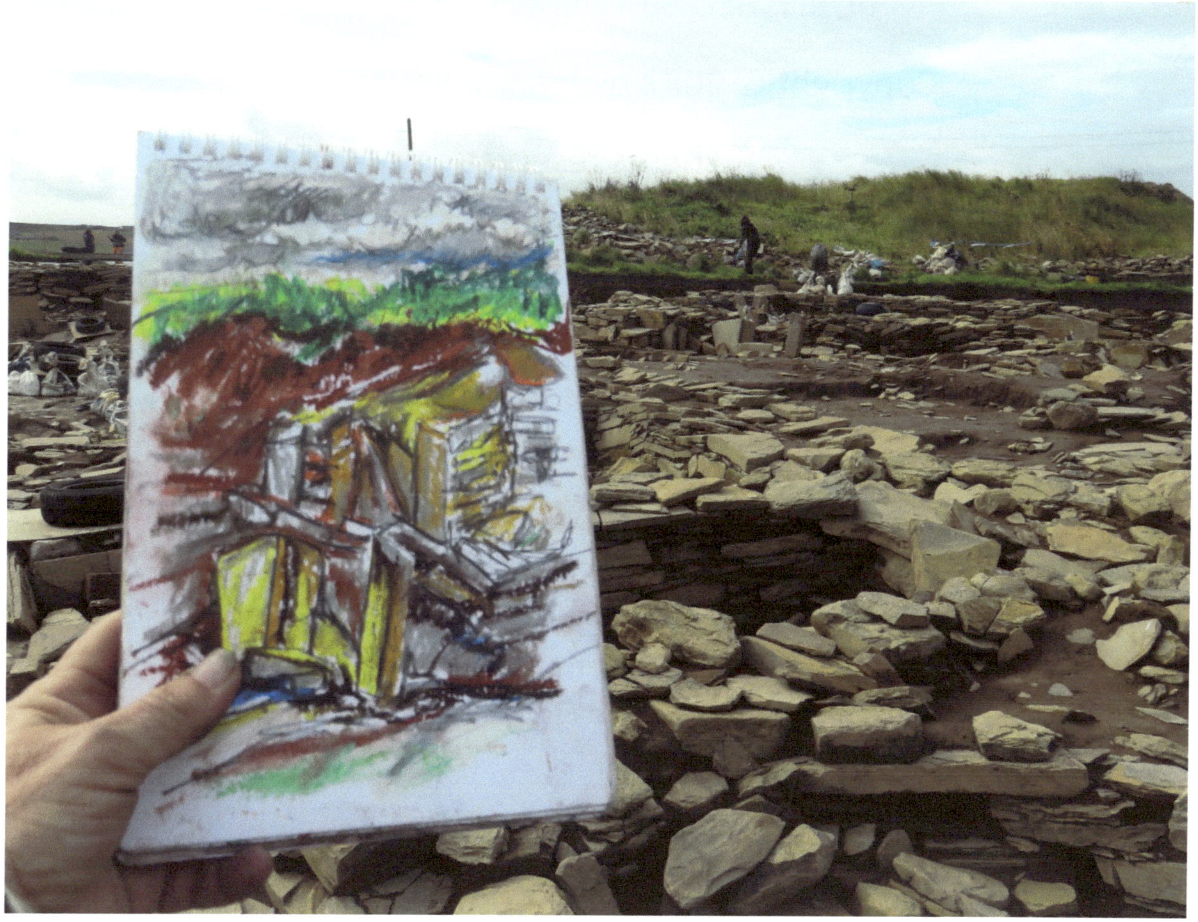

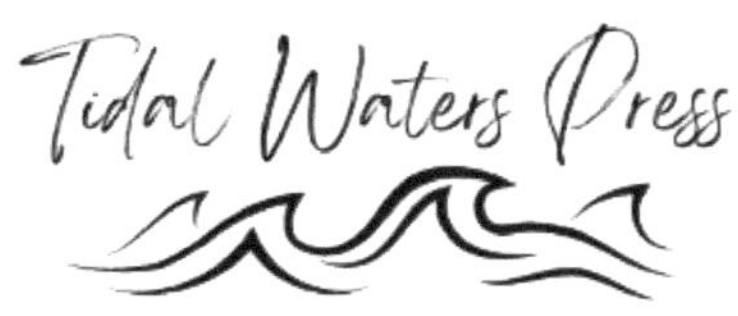

PUBLISHED by Tidal Waters Press

Copyright © 2023 by Jeanne Bouza Rose

All rights reserved.

Paperback edition ISBN 978-1-959318-10-1

https://tidalwaterspress.com

All inquiries should be addressed to **TidalWatersPress.com**

I dedicate this book to Nick Card who finally said "Yes" to me in 2011 and thus started my summer work at the Ness and to Anne Mitchell, who took me on board within the small finds.

And to my sister, who is the writer and publisher in my life! xx

Introduction

In 2018, I was invited to be one of the artists-in-residence at the Ness of Brodgar archaeological excavation in Orkney. Having been a volunteer there since 2011, I was thrilled to paint alongside Karen Wallis in the "art hut," a 15 foot long portacabin. Having plenty of room in the unexpected spacious space, I painted a 15 ft long painting that included portions added with the participation of visiting diggers and archaeologists. (You can purchase a small version of this painting at the Ness of Brodgar online shop.) How would I work the next season after all this size and space?

In 2019, I began to use small canvas boards that I could hold as I worked my way around the trench with my paints. But I needed to reduce the size of the supplies I brought around the edges with me. I do not have a favoured media, so I brought a variety of drawing materials to choose from: watercolour, oil pastel, oil paint sticks, tube oil colours, pigment sticks, and powdered pigment.

The sketches featured here were started accidentally. The weather often dictates what materials I choose, and one day, with a grey sky looming, a small pad and oil pastels seemed worth a try. Working between raindrops, I put two pictures on a page with different orientations. Unlike the archaeologists I paint alongside, I am not particularly accurate with recording my location in pencil. I used my phone photographs and the view behind the sketches to establish the locations.

On site, I noted important information about the area I was looking at in my rather messy handwriting on the back of each sketch. You will find this information typed on the opposite page from the artwork it describes as well as relevant photographs. I hope this helps you understand better what I was seeing.

Although these are rough images meant as a way of planning colour and form for later works and works still to come, I hope they bring you some sense of the site and my particular manner of interpreting it.

I am ever so grateful to all the kindness of the folks at the site and the diggers who work so diligently "over the edges" of the trenches. - Jeanne Bouza Rose

Over the Edge at the Ness of Brodgar

Oil Pastels and earth pigments July Working on site in 2019

All created plein air, between rain, wind and sun

These are photos of the actual artworks in my sketchbook—Jeanne Bouza Rose

Looking across Str.12.
to entrance looking east

LOOKING ACROSS STRUCTURE 12
TO ITS ENTRANCE. LOOKING EAST

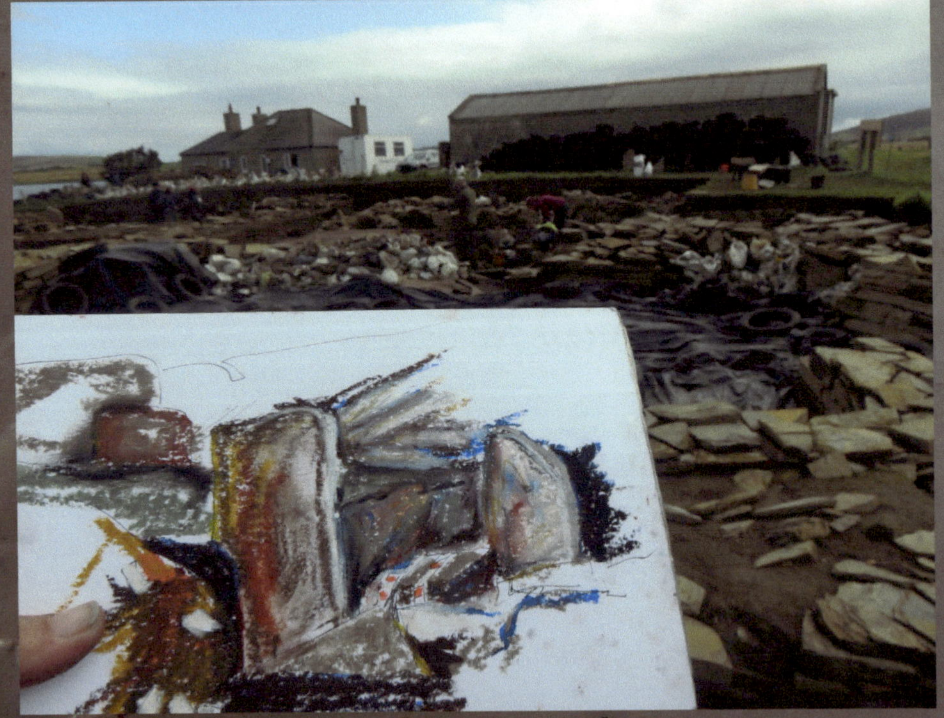

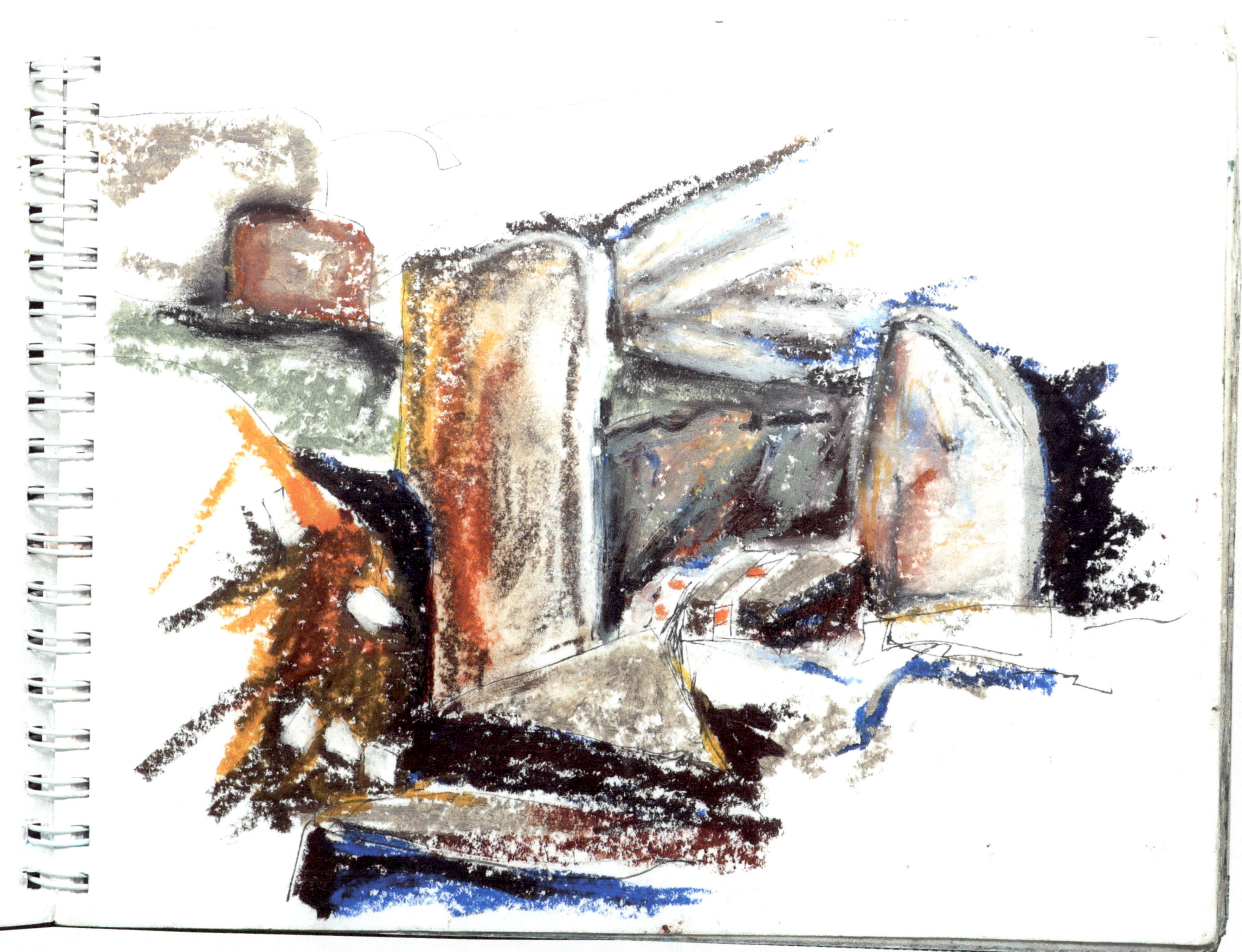

ON THE EDGE OF 12 LOOKING AT THE EDGE OF 8? THE CURVE

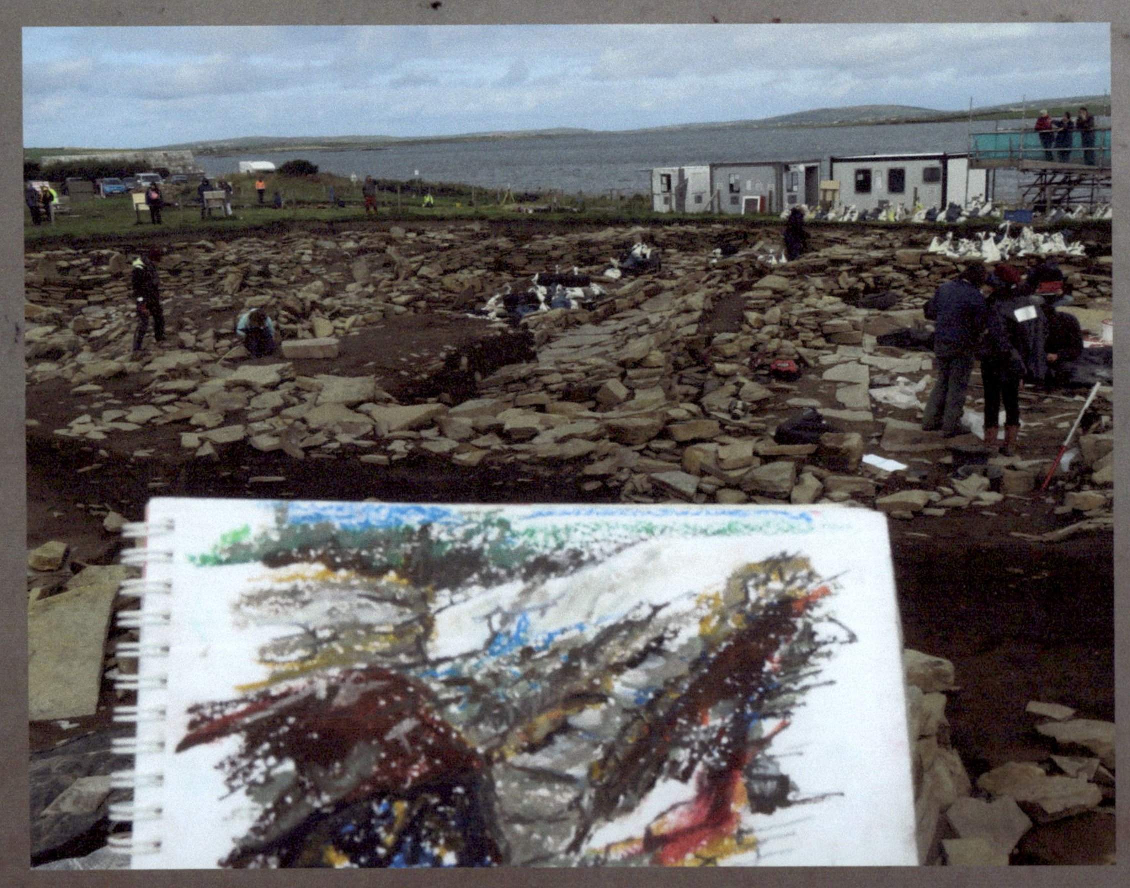

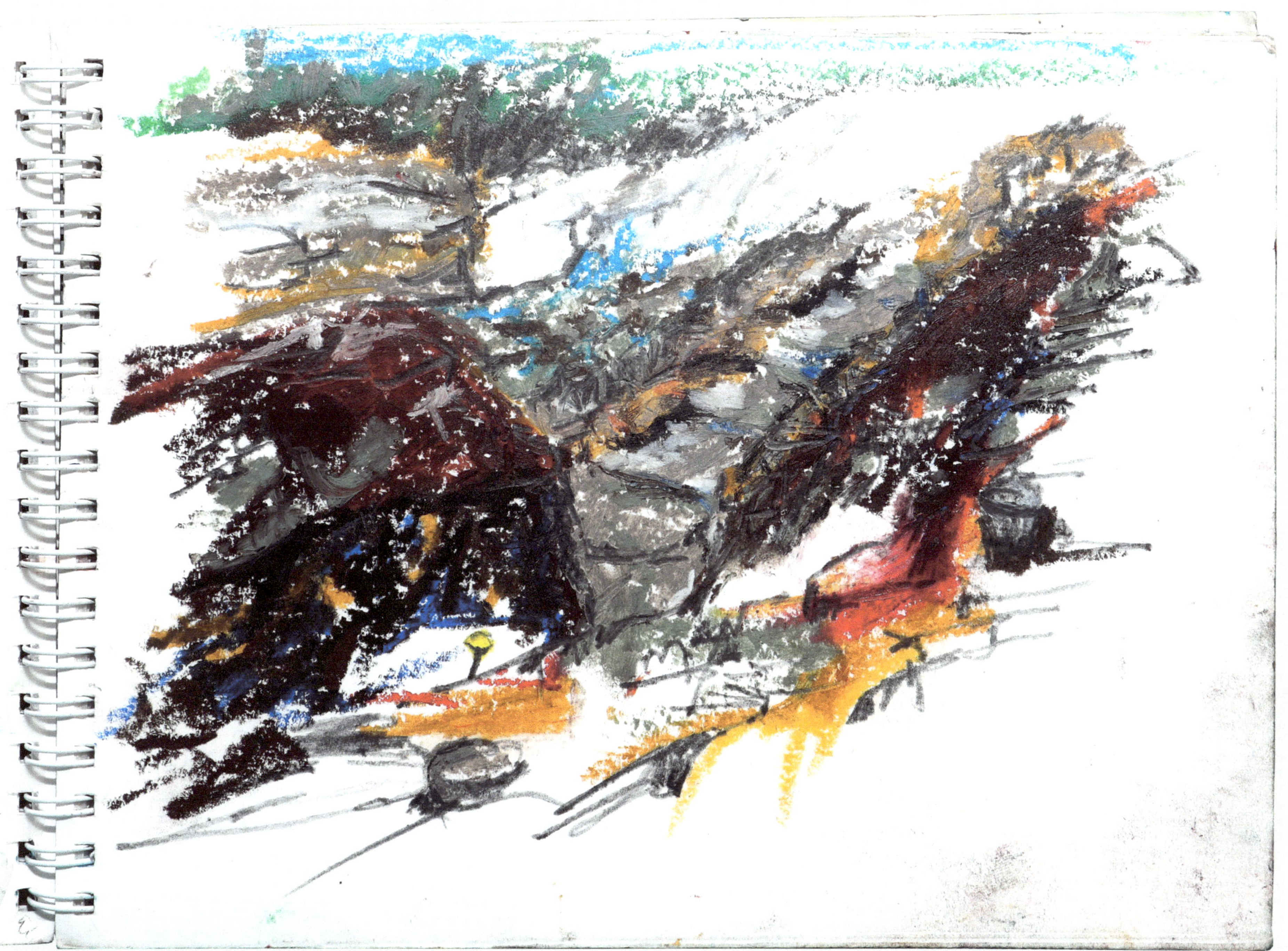

On some days, you can see the full view of the Stenness Loch with the Hoy hills in the background. On this day, I could see the two hills beyond the main lines of Hoy. It was a special moment.

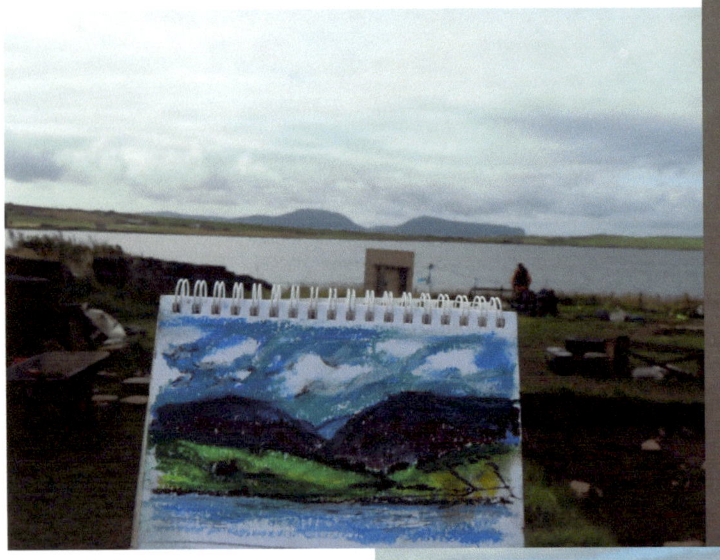

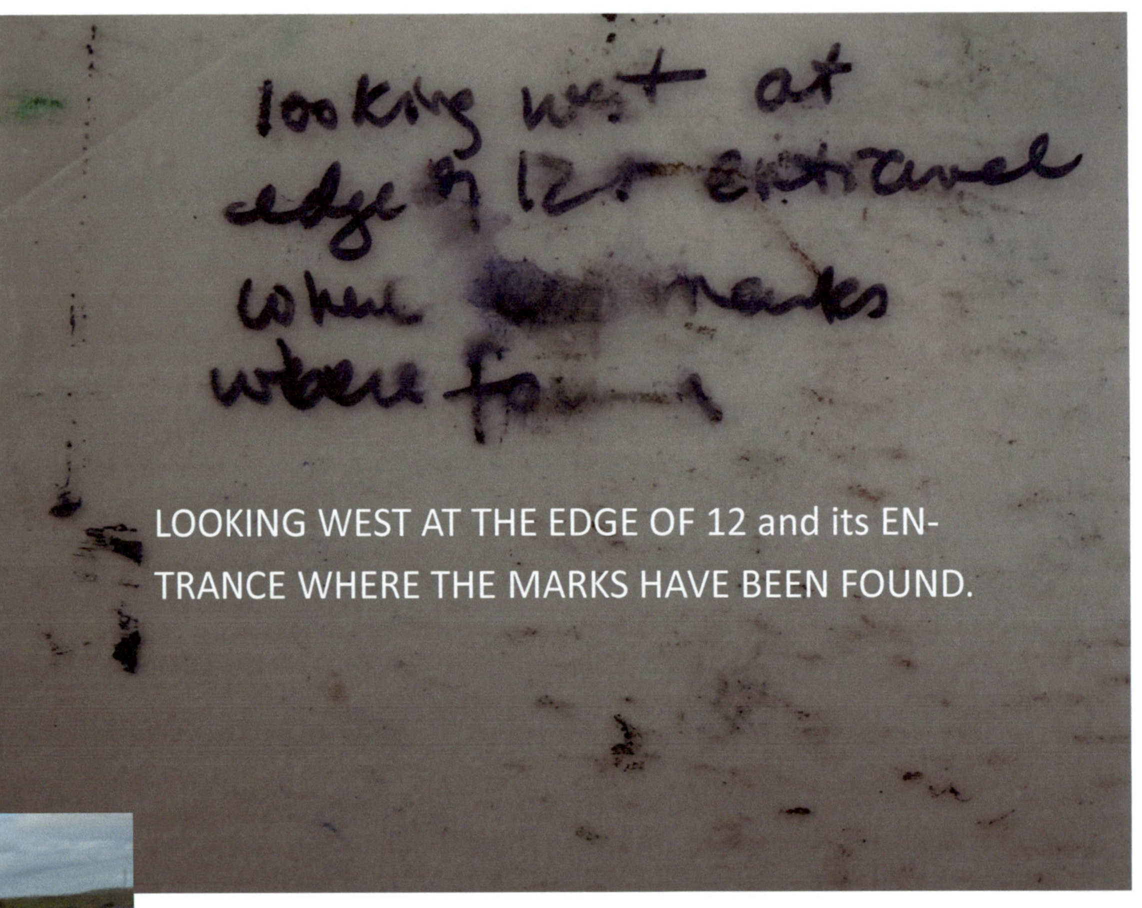

LOOKING WEST AT THE EDGE OF 12 and its EN-TRANCE WHERE THE MARKS HAVE BEEN FOUND.

Looking across the eastern edge of Structure 12 towards the spoil heap. Just over the top of the larger orthostat on the right, I focused in on this this area . Another orthostat lies opposite and creates an entrance.

Before the end of the season, interesting incised stones were uncovered and a quern stone was found. Turns out I am often painting a view that ends up being a place of interest. Hmm...

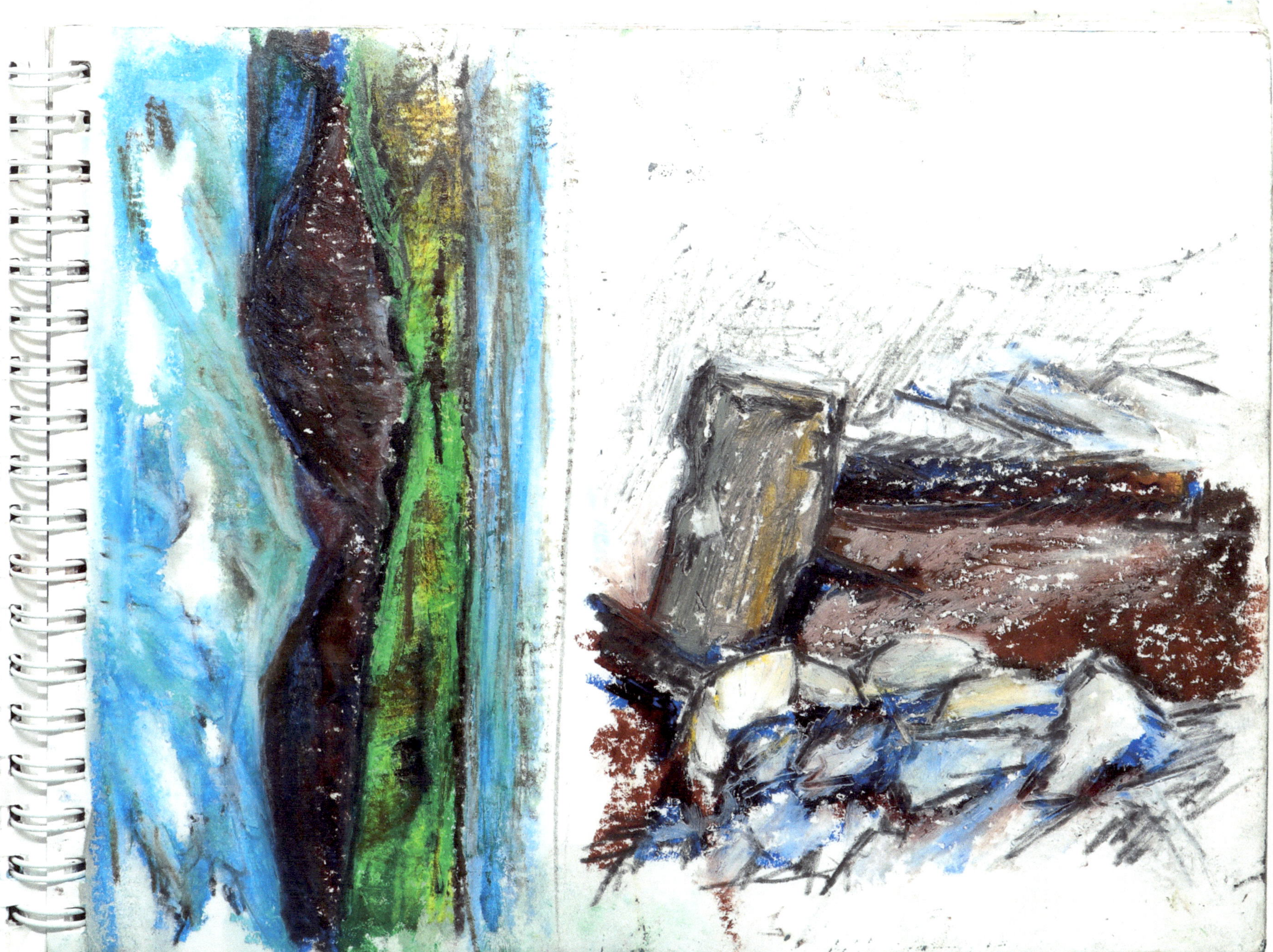

A bit along
Stru 8
pavement.

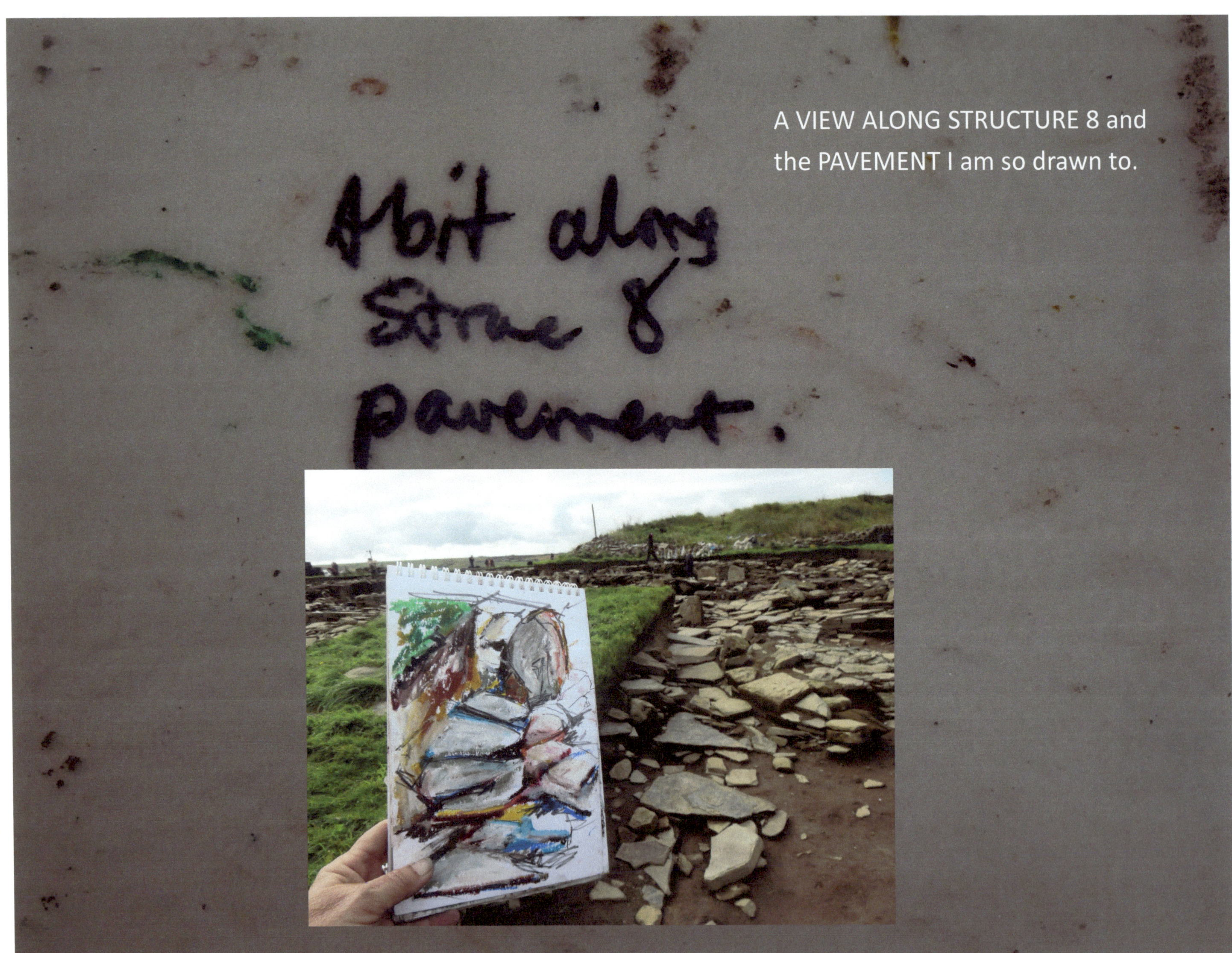

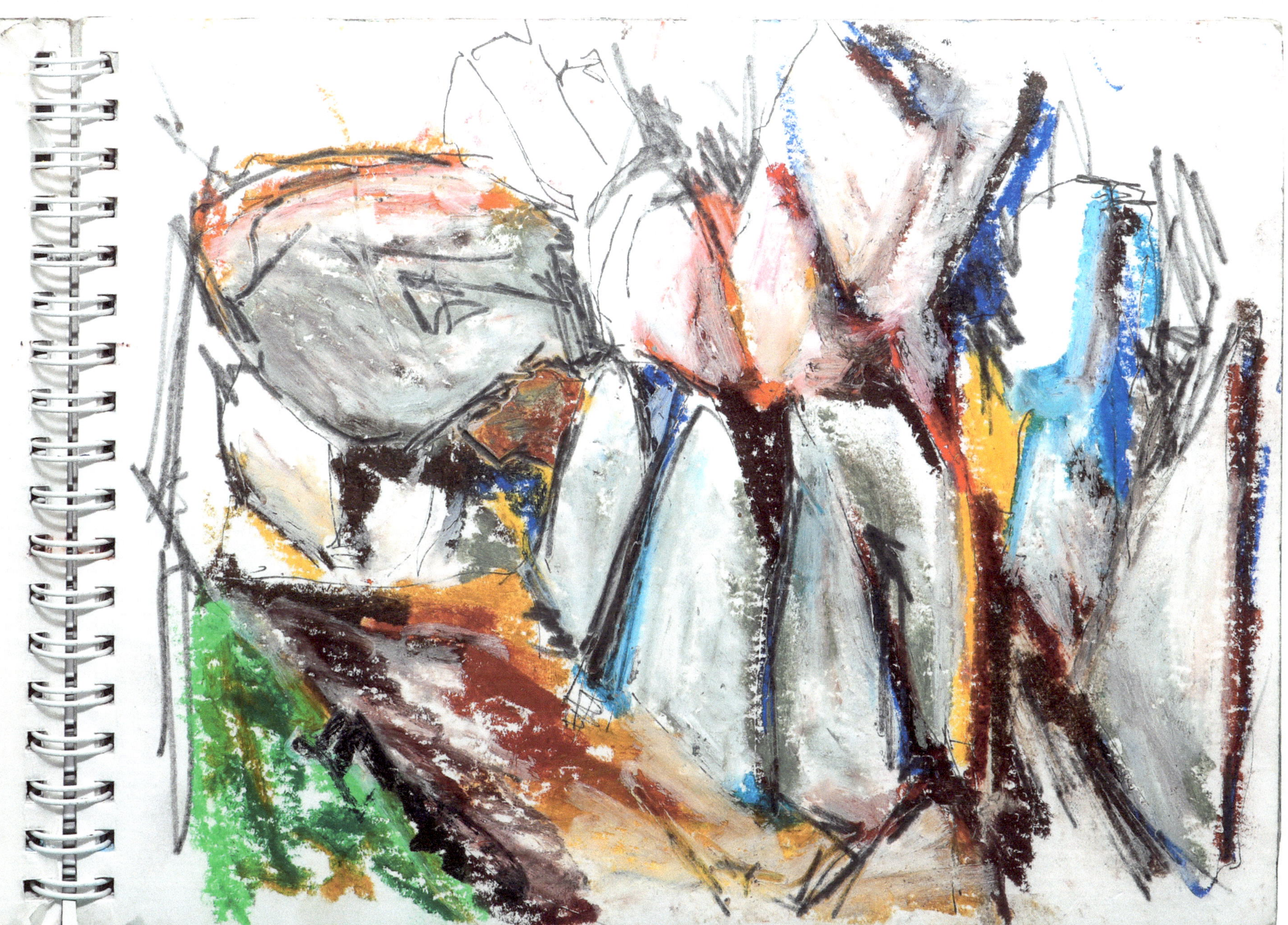

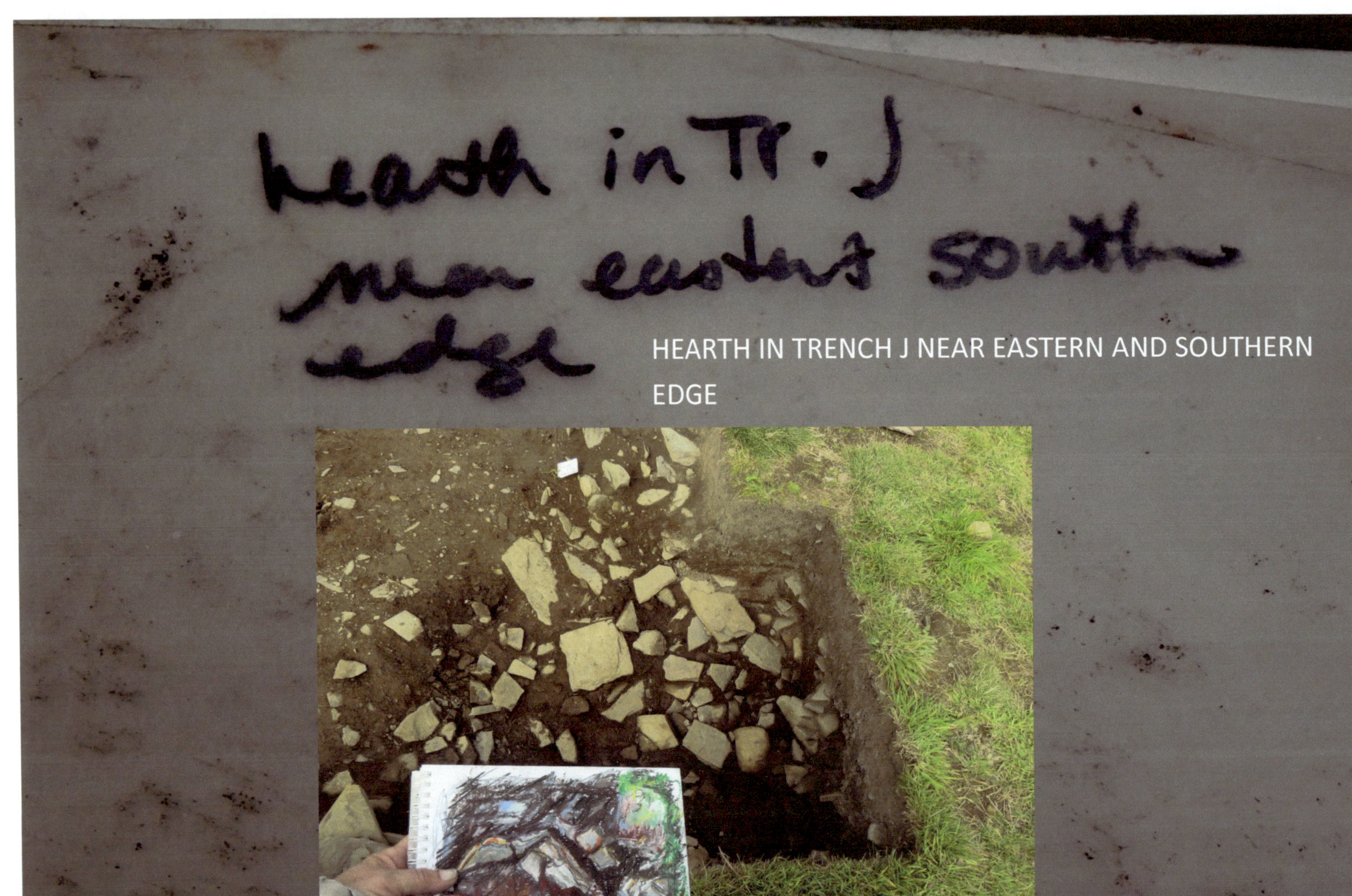

HEARTH IN TRENCH J NEAR EASTERN AND SOUTHERN EDGE

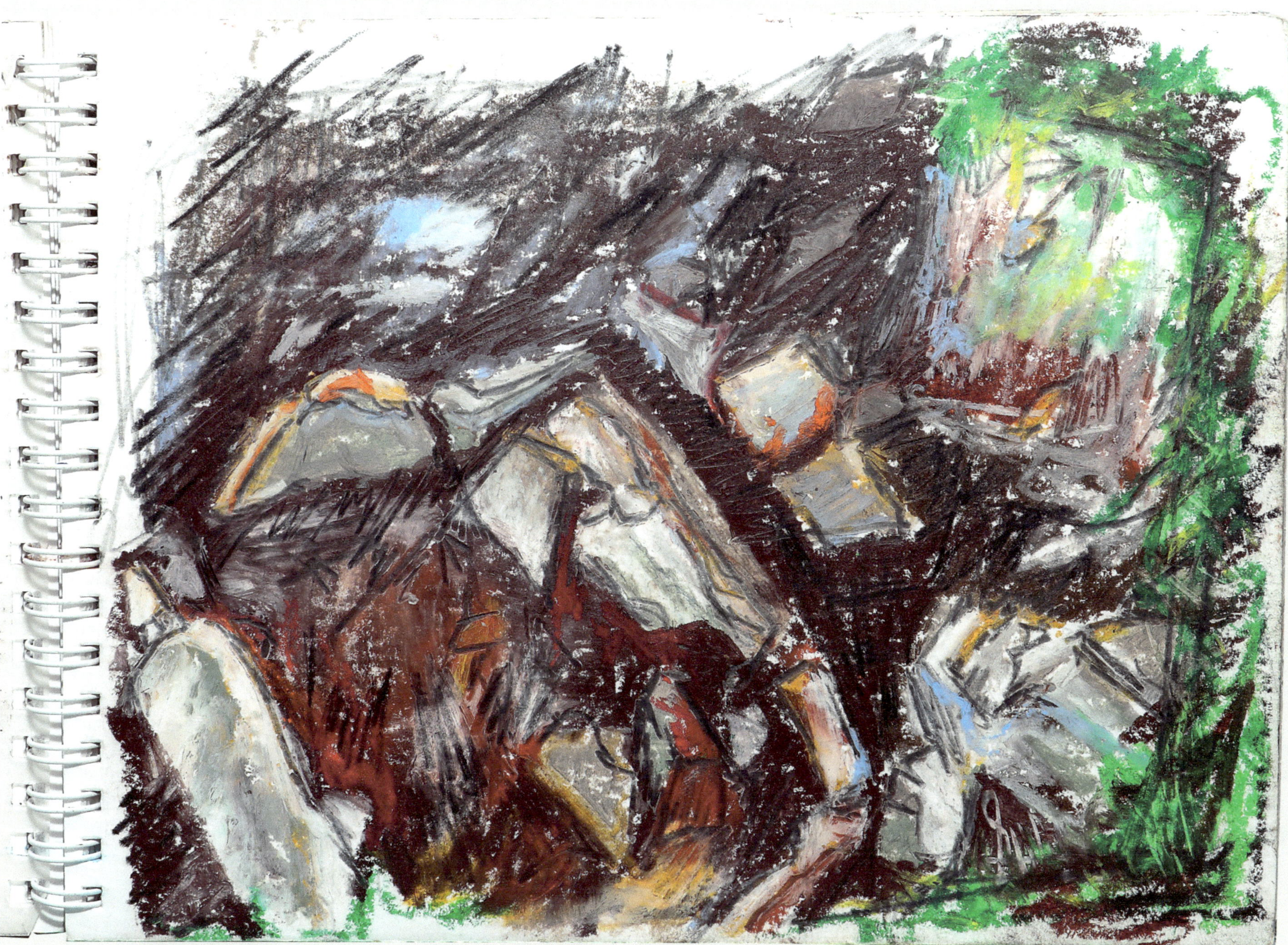

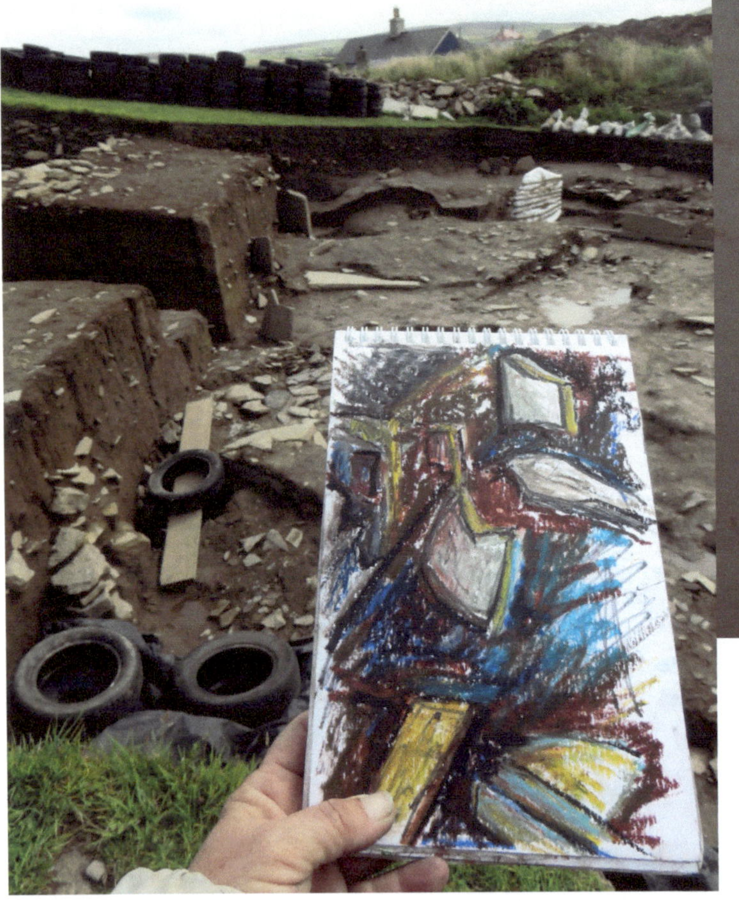

The 3 large stones
in Tr. T.

THE 3 LARGE STONES IN TRENCH T

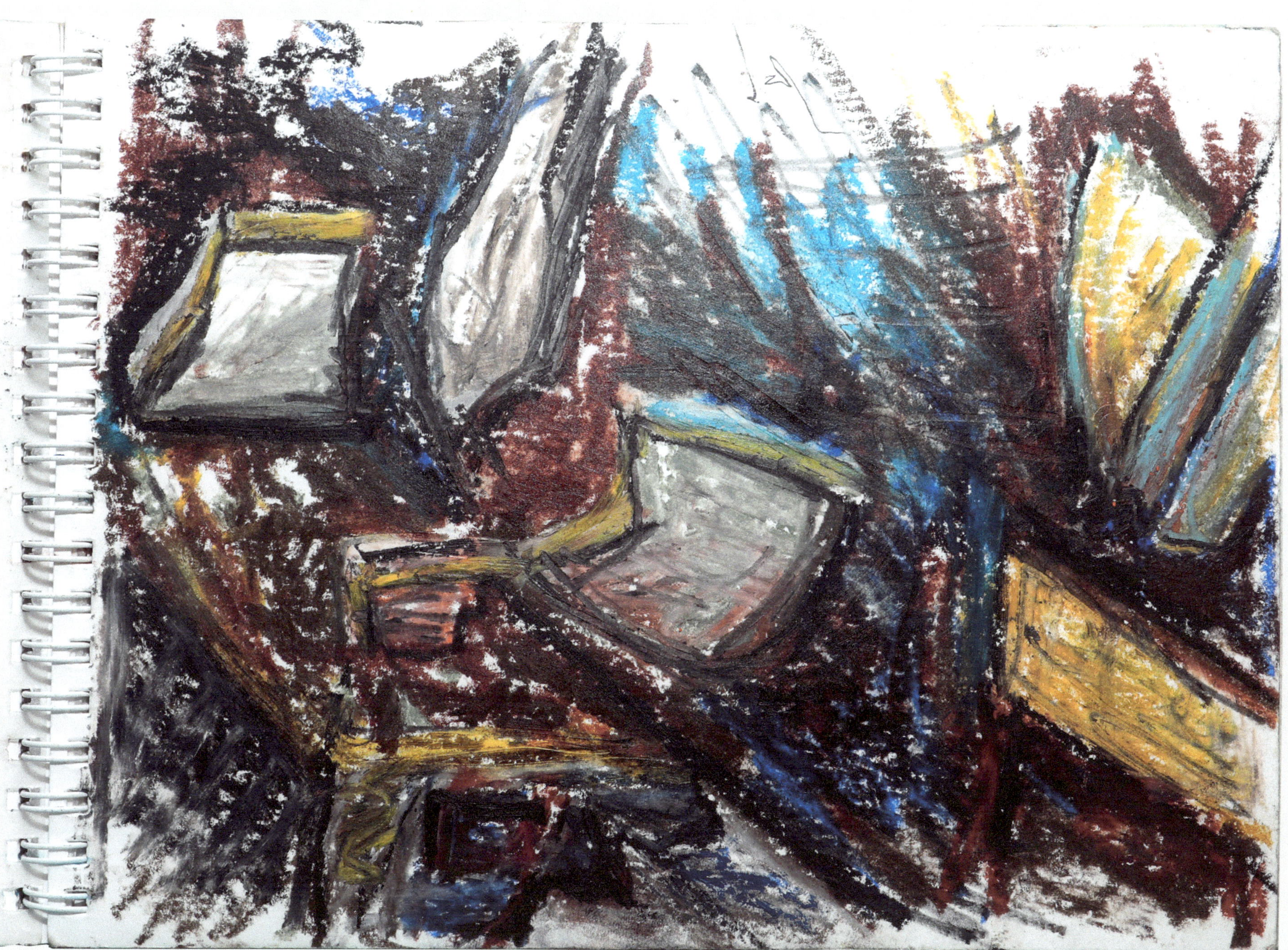

ACROSS FROM the
NORTHERN EDGE SEEING
THE ENTRANCE TO
STRUCTURE 1 ?

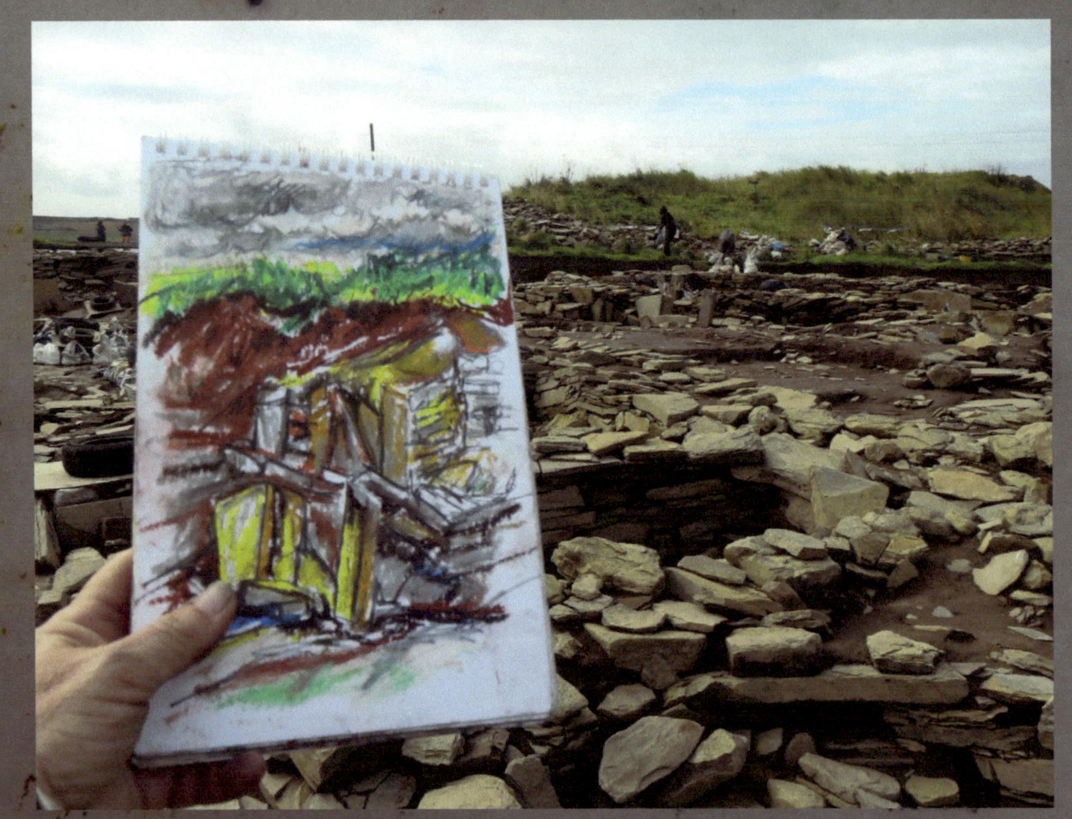

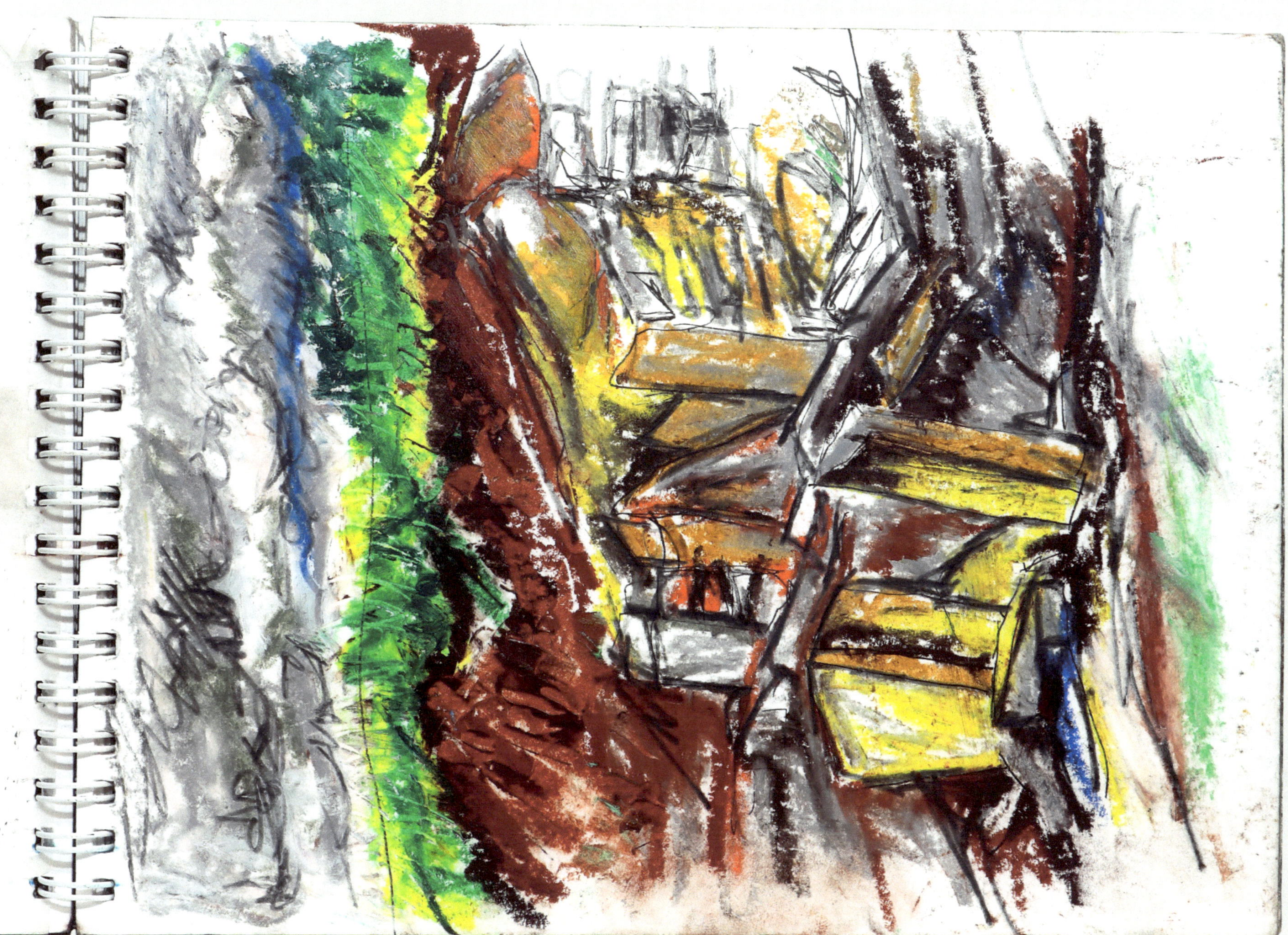

SPLADONGAS is the name I was give permission to create by Dr. Jo McKenzie, the site micromorphologist. It is a new word to describe the rectangular recesses left after a KUBIENA sample has been taken. Technically, it is a Specific Point Location so....
SPL-adonga. I was fascinated by the design of these recesses and drew them frequently enough that they needed a name.

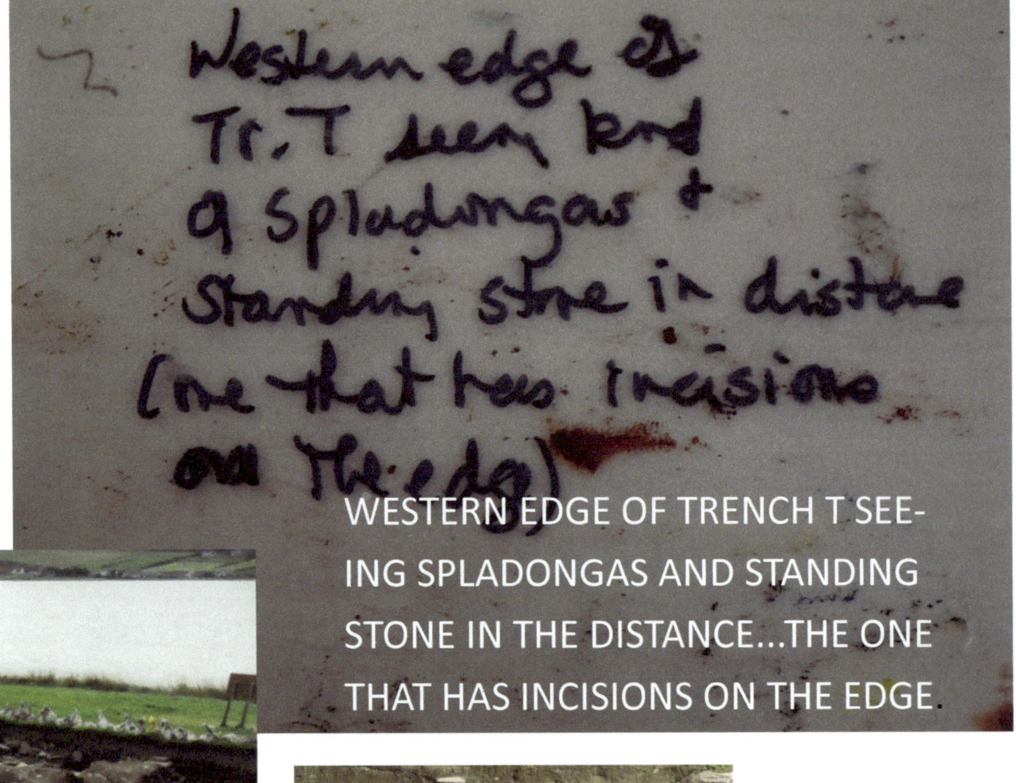

WESTERN EDGE OF TRENCH T SEEING SPLADONGAS AND STANDING STONE IN THE DISTANCE...THE ONE THAT HAS INCISIONS ON THE EDGE.

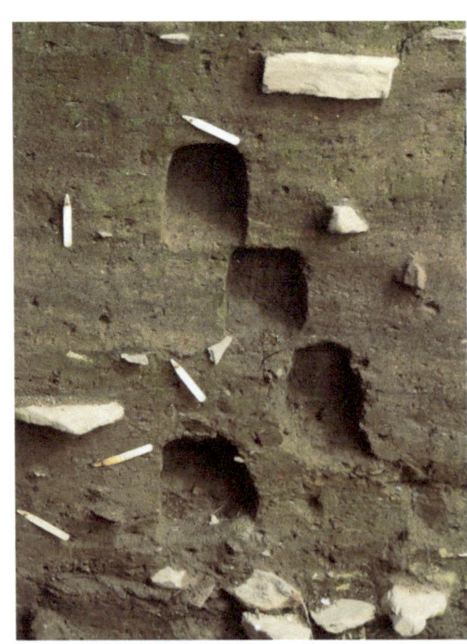

The SPLADONGA Recesses.

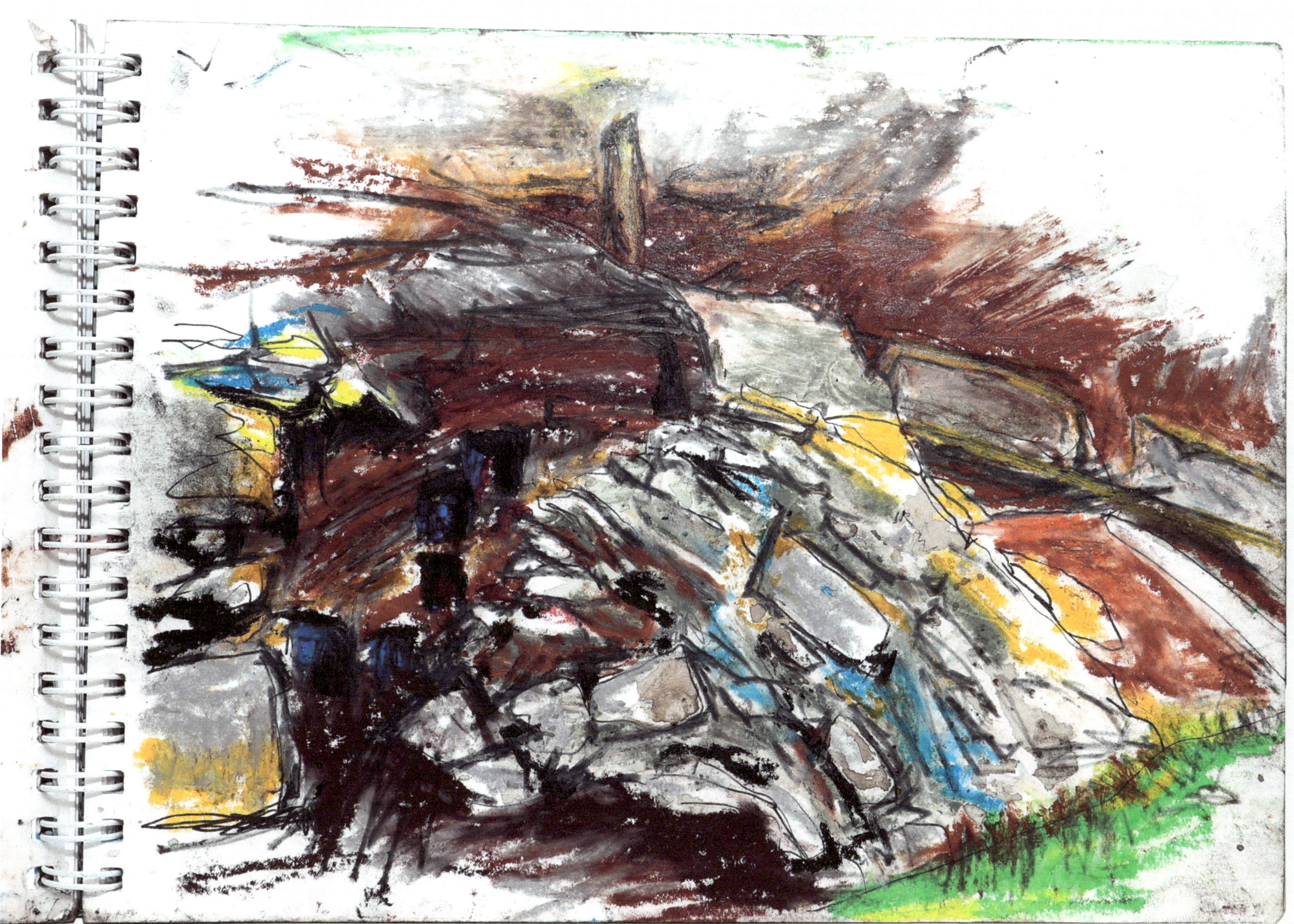

View of Stenn
from edge of Tr. T
west

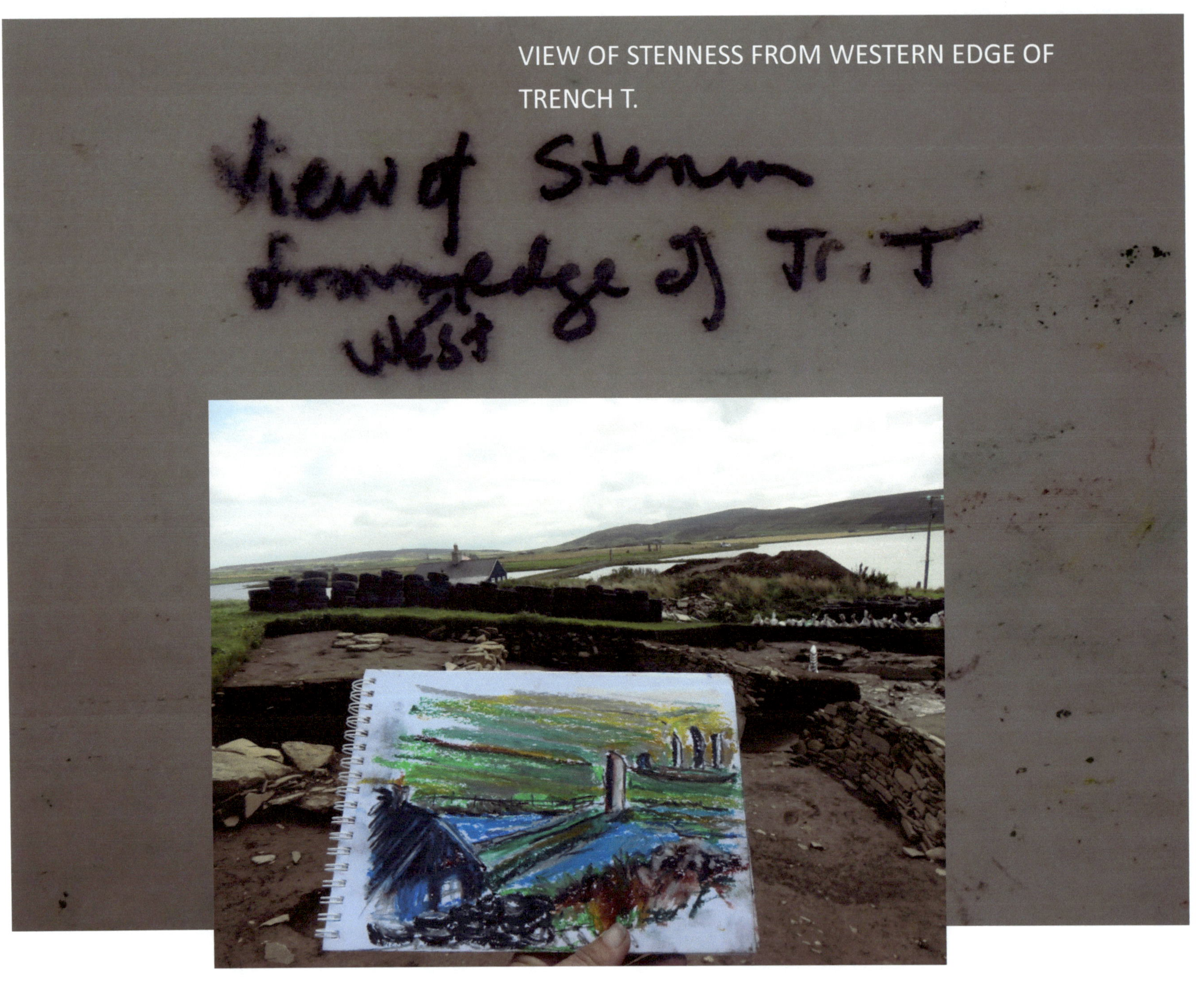

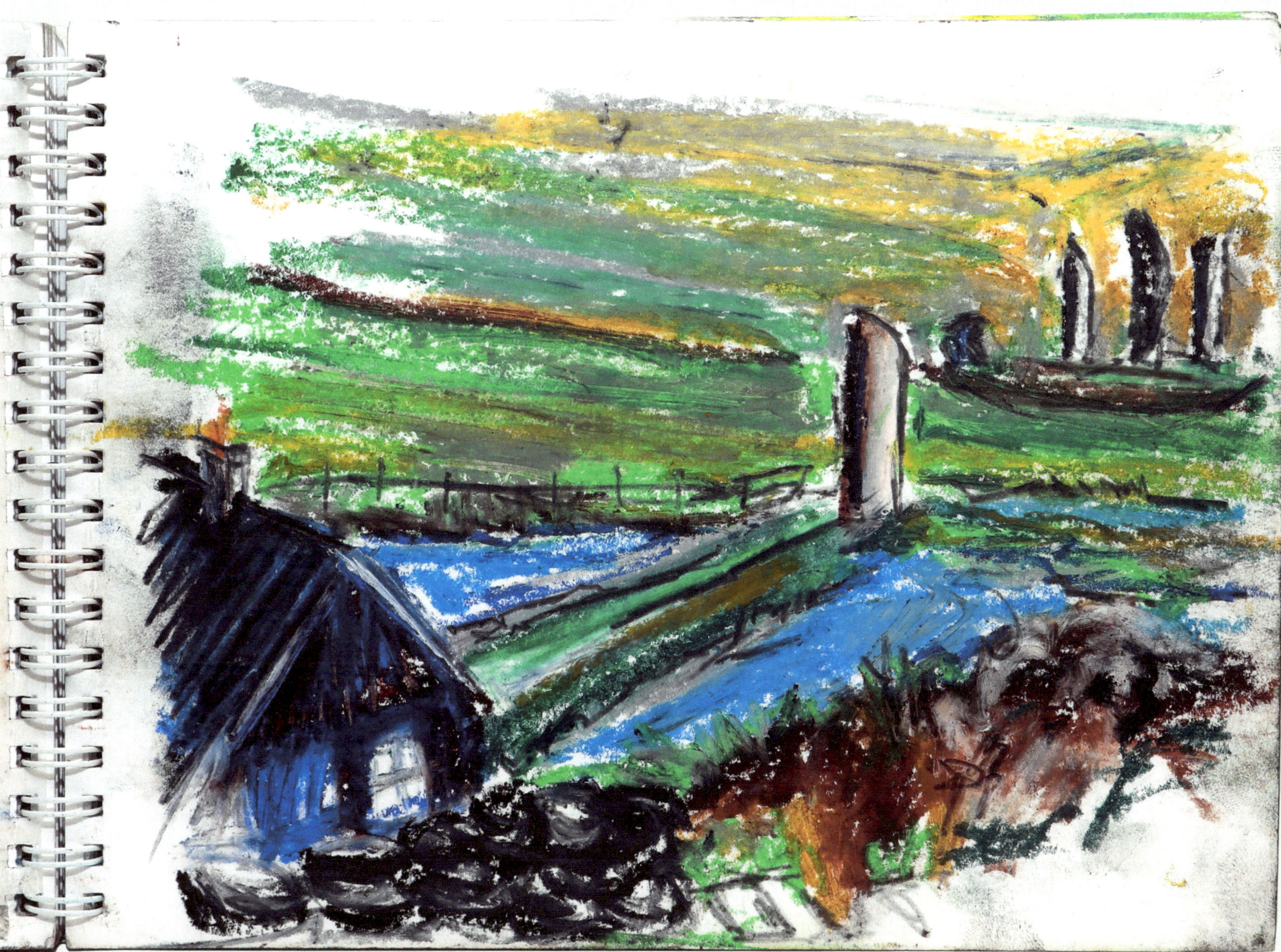

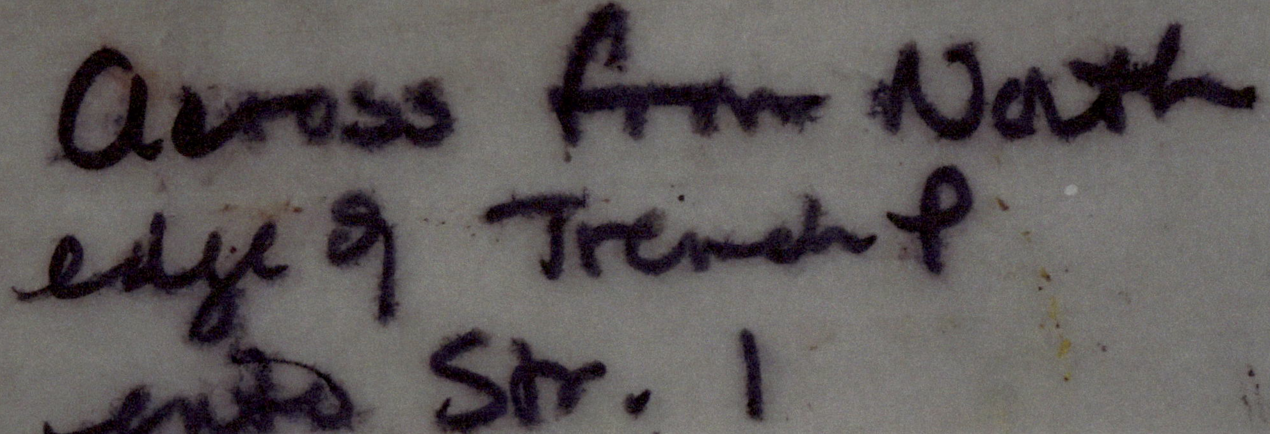

Across from North
edge of Trench P
into Str. 1

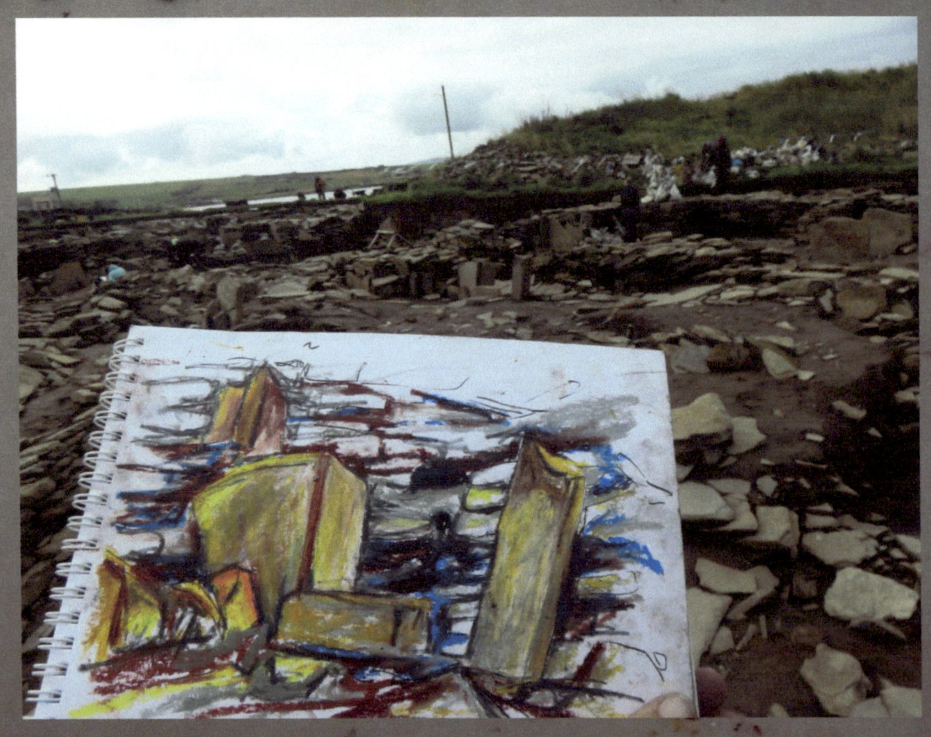

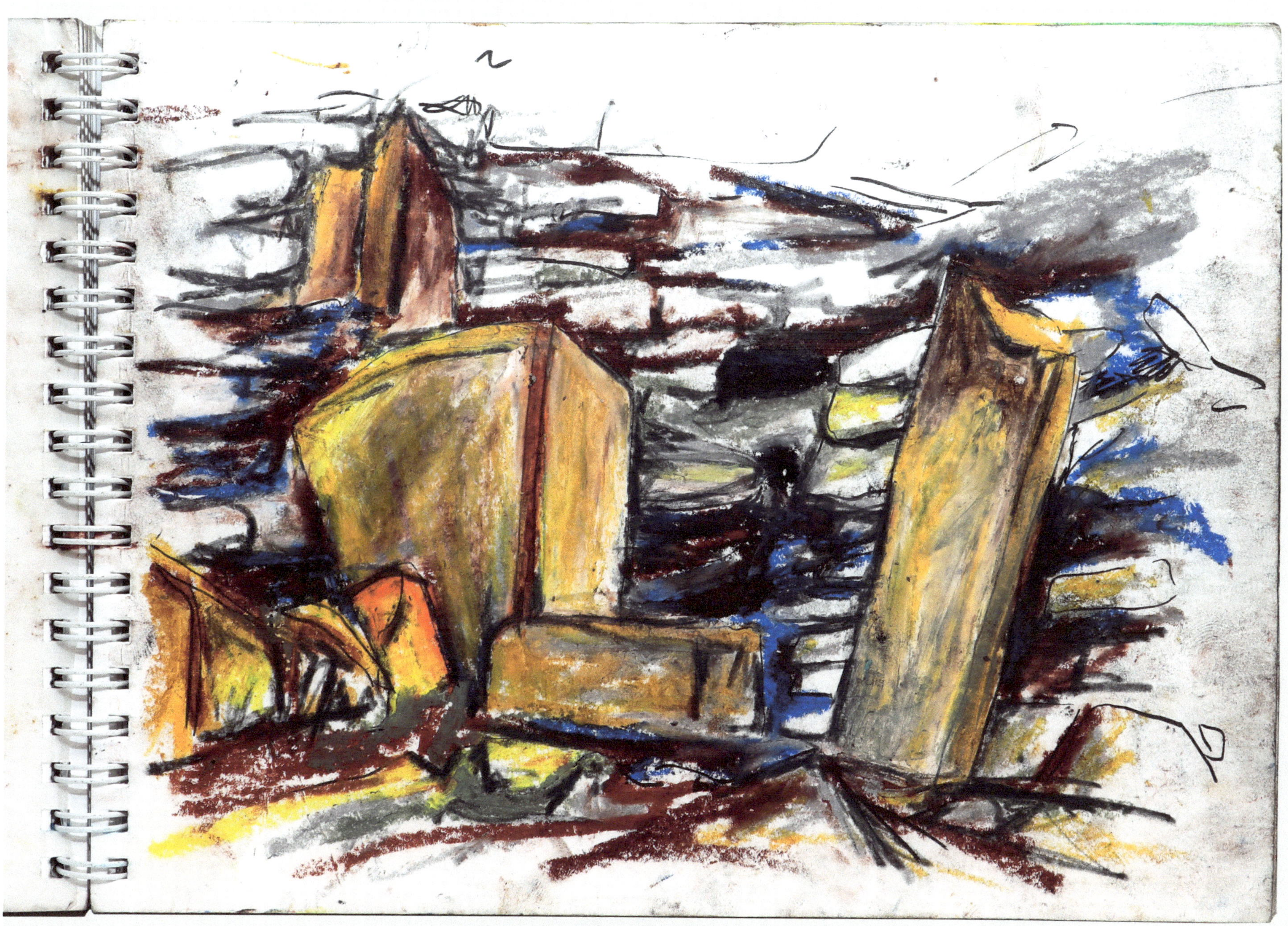

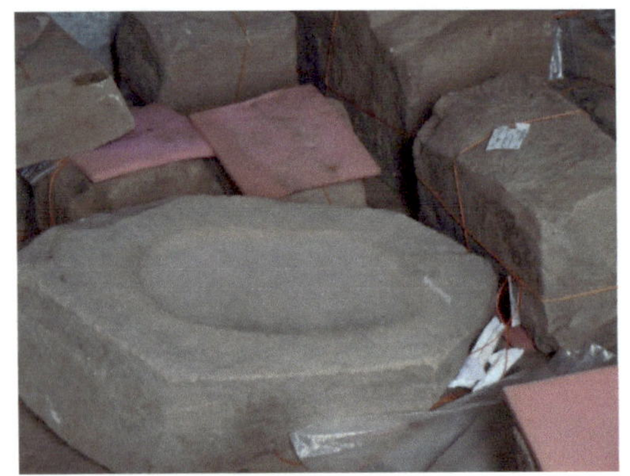

A quern stone was found in the wall of this "entrance" area.

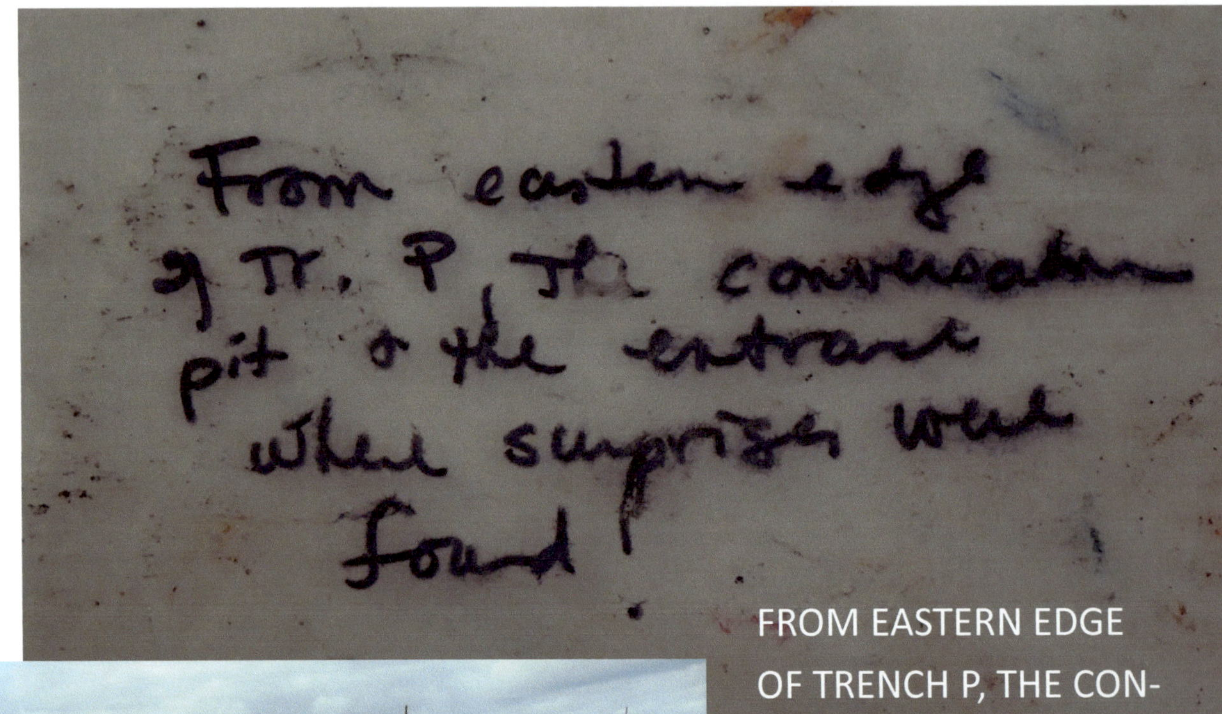

FROM EASTERN EDGE OF TRENCH P, THE CONVERSATION PIT AND THE ENTRANCE WHERE SURPRISES WERE FOUND.

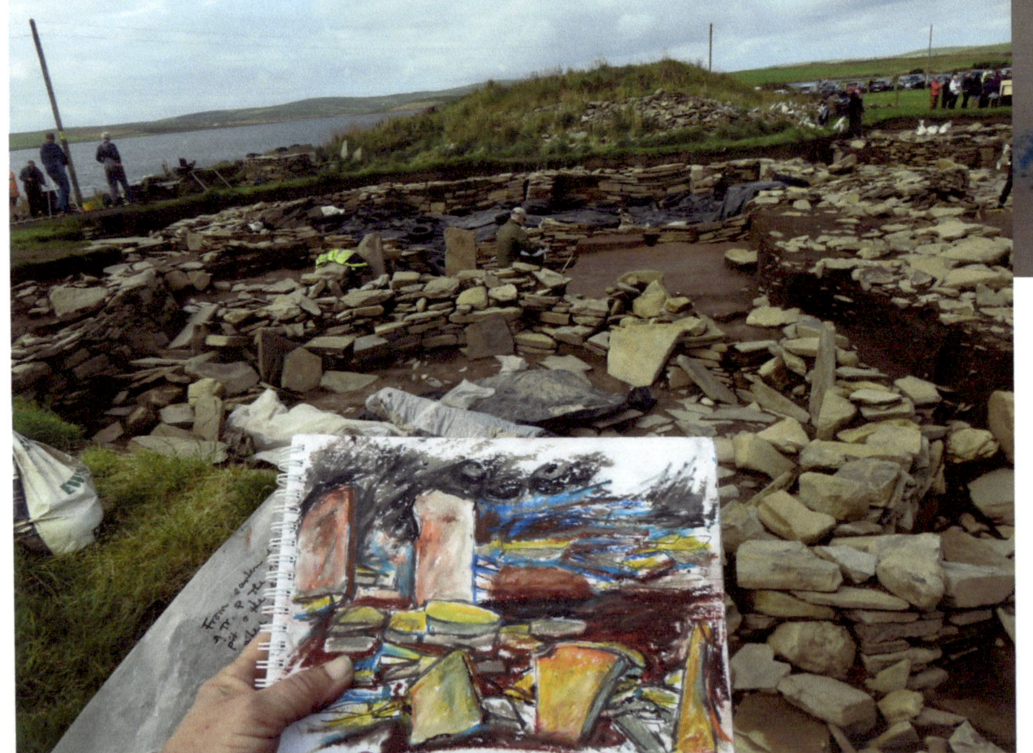

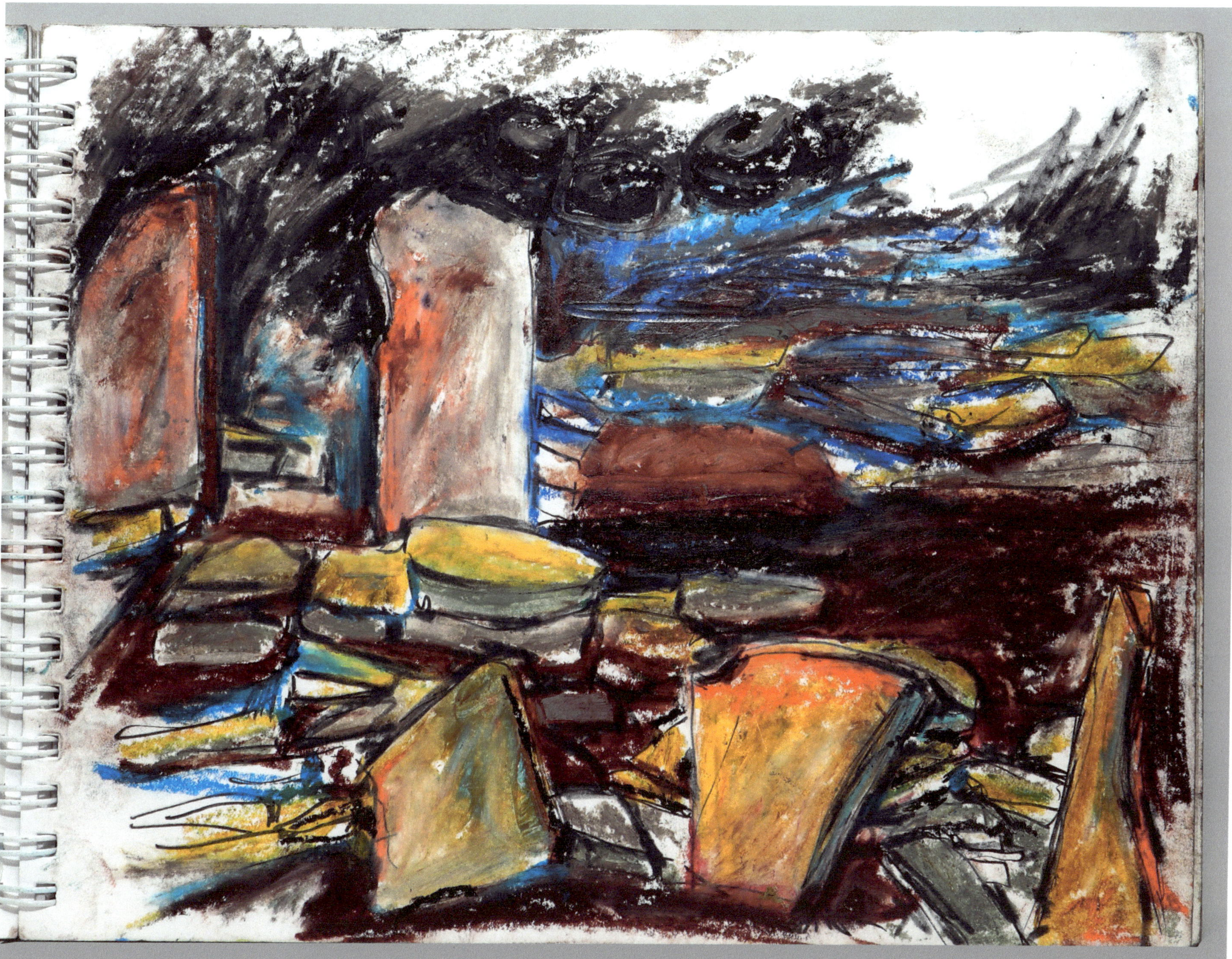

Trench 6
Fire
Sitting at nor
end –
Swath
of sondage
still anchor
to wall

TRENCH J OVERLOOKING STRUCTURE 5 SITTING AT THE NORTH END - A SWATH OF SONDAGE STILL ATTACHED TO WALL

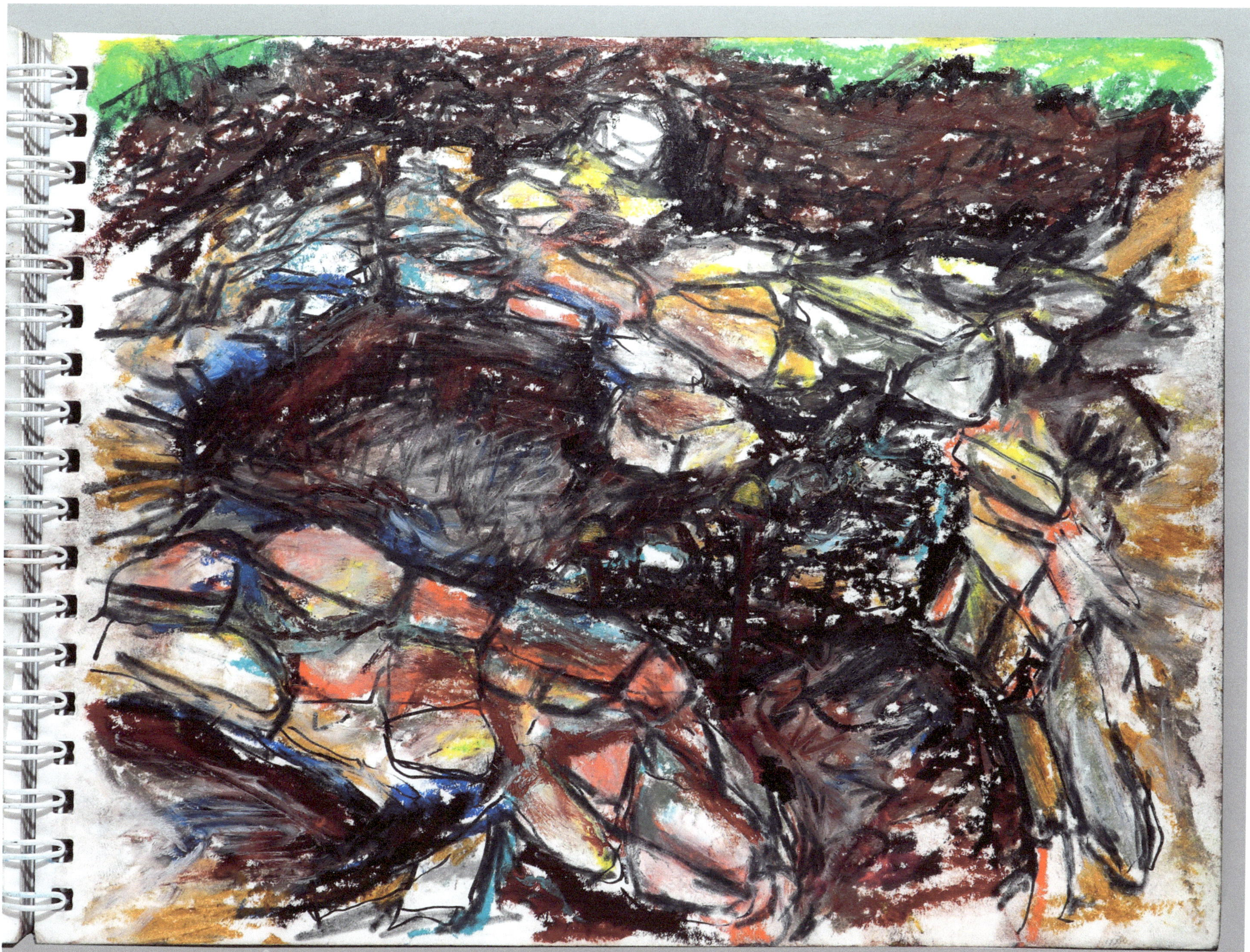

www.ingramcontent.com/pod-product-compliance
Lightning Source LLC
Chambersburg PA
CBHW042033050726

47599CB00006B/887